art in focus

Hilary Ansell

Acknowledgements

I would like to thank the children from Kingfisher Primary School whose work has been photographed for this book. Thank you for your interest and enthusiasm.

Thank you also to my great friends at St. John's Hospice and The Oaks Centre for all your support and encouragement and to Doncaster Museum Loan Service for the use of my Woodland Path Collage on page 41.

Above all, a big thank you to my husband Andrew who took over all household duties for two months whilst I went into creative hibernation in the attic. Thanks for putting up with me!

'Clay Relief Roofscape' (page 13)

© 2002 Folens on behalf of the author.

Belair Publications, Apex Business Centre, Boscombe Road, Dunstable, LU5 4RL.
Email: belair@belair-publications.co.uk

Commissioning Editor: Karen McCaffery   Editor: Elizabeth Miles/Jennifer Steele
Page Layout: Suzanne Ward   Cover Design: Steve West   Illustrator: Hilary Ansell

Photography: Right-hand pages Kelvin Freeman
              Left-hand pages   Hilary Ansell
              Page 12 (bottom) Aerial View of Flat-Roofed Buildings   © Yann Arthus-Bertrand/Corbis
              Page 14 (bottom)   © Corel
              Page 16 (bottom) Sun Setting over Pacific Ocean   © James Randklev/Corbis
              Page 18 (top) Snowy Road in Glen Prosen, Scotland   © Terry Whittaker; Frank Lane Picture Agency/Corbis
              Page 26 (top) Aerial View of Patchwork Field   © Yann Arthus-Bertrand/Corbis
              Page 28 Felled trees, page 62 Seaweed   Dennis Hepworth
              Page 30 (bottom) Gears   © Lawrence Manning/Corbis
              Page 58 (bottom) La Géode, Paris   David Binnington
              Page 68 (top) Still life with jugs   Kelvin Freeman

First published in 2002 by Belair Publications.
Revised edition 2005 © Belair Publishers

British Library Cataloguing in Publication Data. A catalogue record for this publication is available from the British Library.

ISBN 0 94788 260 X

Contents

Introduction

When considering design work, the most important starting point is to learn to look. The aim of this book is to encourage children to look and to 'see' in order to develop an awareness of pattern, shape, colour and texture in the local environment and to use this enhanced awareness to develop their artwork.

Use a camera to develop the art of looking and selecting. Look through the camera's viewfinder and examine what you see, from top to bottom, from side to side and from corner to corner. Try other camera angles, squat down, stand on something or even lie down if it's possible but fill the frame with the subject. Go in close. The picture will have more impact if you do. Look for lines such as paths, hedgerows and hills that lead the eye into the photograph. Try to include a foreground such as a gate, wall or slope of grass to emphasise the perspective of the view.

Consider also whether the photograph is best taken in landscape or portrait format. It is so easy to take photographs with wasted space at either side of the subject when it would have been better to turn the camera around to make the subject fill the frame. All the points of composition, which help to create an interesting photograph, apply when choosing the subject for a landscape sketch, painting or collage.

When taking photographs of landscapes, try not to cut the picture exactly in half with the horizon. The photograph will be more interesting with different proportions of sky and land. Remember also that strong overhead sunlight in the middle of the day tends to flatten out the contours of landscapes. Later in the day, when the sunlight is sloping across the landscape at an angle, it creates more shadows and emphasises texture.

Because 'selecting' the subject is such an important factor in creating interesting photographs and artwork, it is a good idea to accustom the children to using a card viewer, as it can often be difficult to isolate interesting arrangements of line and shape from the wider background.

To make a card viewer simply cut out a 7cm x 5cm rectangle from the centre of a slightly larger piece of card. Use this to compose subjects for drawings and paintings. Encourage the children to view things from unusual angles and record their findings in sketchbooks. They will become aware of the fact that the nearer the viewer is to the subject, the more the subject fills the frame and conversely if they draw back from the subject it appears to take up less space in the frame. When recording what they see in the viewer they need to be aware of proportion, that is, how the lines of the subject divide the space within the rectangle.

Once confident in selecting a subject it is time to start creating a permanent record of it. Digital cameras are excellent because the photographs can be taken, viewed, then either erased or downloaded and printed on the computer. Multiple copies can be printed in a variety of sizes. Alternatively, disposable cameras are a relatively cheap option and prove to be useful when several groups of children are working at the same time.

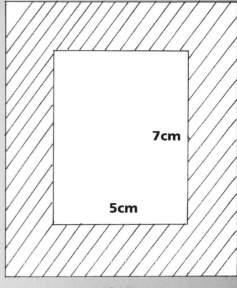

Card viewer

In most instances the photographs will act as an *aide-mémoire*, providing an opportunity to study the subject more closely and for as long as necessary. Look for line, form, texture and colour within the photographs and consider how best to portray these through collage, fabric, paint or clay.

Hopefully, through the process of looking and selecting appropriate media, the children will become more aware of line, shape, colour and texture in their surroundings, but the most important thing of all is to have fun and enjoy what they are doing!

5

Doors and Doorways

Buildings in the local environment can provide a rich source of study for texture, pattern and shape. Look closely at the doors and doorways in the neighbourhood. Do you think that some doors look more attractive than others? Why is this? Do some doors have glass or decorative panelling? Are the doors an indication of the age of the building? Older doorways often feature decorative carved wood or stonework. Use a camera to record such details for future work on pattern and shape.

Ideas Board

Resources
- Photographs of doors
- White card
- Wax crayons
- Coloured inks
- Photographs
- Glue

Approach

1. Create an ideas board using photographs of interesting doorways in the local area. Look for unusual patterns in woodwork or stonework around the doorways.

2. Create a background by lightly crayoning in different colours over white card, using the side of the wax crayons.

3. Colour wash over the crayon in different coloured inks.

4. Cut out doorways and interesting features from the photograph collection.

5. Arrange these on the background and glue into position.

Doorways in Clay

Resources
- Clay
- Slip
- Clay tools

Approach

1. Roll out a slab of clay between two wooden guides to ensure an even thickness (1.5 to 2cm).

2. Cut out a rectangle of clay about 22 x 17cm.

3. Select an interesting doorway from the ideas board and begin to build up the features of the doorway in the clay.

4. Cut narrow strips of clay for the architrave around the doors and remember to 'glue' all additions with water or slip.

5. Build up the doorstep and add details, such as flower tubs or pieces of sculpture.

6. Finally, incise patterns of brick and stonework around the doorway using clay tools.

Windows

Windows are to be found in all shapes and sizes and can provide an interesting starting point for imaginative work. The view through a window depends on whether you are looking in or looking out. Compare the windows of old and new buildings. Which have the larger windows? Why? How many different patterns of window can be seen along one street? Often in older areas the window frames are more ornate. Look for patterned brick or stonework above the windows.

Stencilled Windows

Resources
- Photographs of windows
- White paper
- Yellow tissue paper
- Cellulose paste
- Thin card
- Stencil brushes
- Paints
- Black oil pastels

Approach

1. Prepare a textured background by pasting crumpled and then smoothed-out yellow tissue paper onto a sheet of white paper. Leave to dry.

2. Cut out window stencils of different shapes and sizes from thin card.

3. Arrange the stencils in an interesting pattern on the background.

4. Stencil over the framework with paint. Do not paint in the whole window shape.

5. When the paint is dry, lightly rub over the picture with a black oil pastel. The wrinkles in the paper will pick up the pastel and create an interesting texture.

Through the Window

Resources
- White paper
- Coloured paper
- Glue
- Glossy magazines
- Scraps of tissue paper and fabric
- Paints

Approach

1. Decide upon a viewpoint, either looking out of a window or looking in.

2. Cut a suitable picture from a magazine and glue it to the white background paper.

3. Cut a window frame from coloured paper and glue into position over the cut-out scene.

4. If desired, add tissue or fabric curtains.

5. Finally, draw and paint in the rest of the wall or scene.

Walls

Photograph a variety of walls that can be seen in the local environment. Note the differences in texture, colour and pattern and use this as a stimulus for work in paint and fabric. If possible, photograph the inside and outside of the same wall and note the effects of pollution and weathering. If the immediate environment is predominantly red brick, extend the collection to include stone and slate walls. Paving can also be included.

Colour Matching

Approach

1. Study photographs of walls or paving. Identify the many shades of colour in them.

2. In pencil, lightly draw the outline of the bricks or stones.

3. Use paint or pastels to recreate as many shades of the wall or paving colours as possible.

Quilted Walls

Resources
- Quilted Walls
- Latex fabric glue
- Wadding
- Materials
- Thin backing fabric
- Sewing thread
- Dark background material
- Stone- and moss-coloured fabrics
- Sewing pins and needles

Approach

1. Cut out brick or stone shapes from appropriately coloured fabrics and glue or sew onto dark background material.

2. Decorate the stones with stitching or scraps of green velvet or velour to represent moss.

3. Place the picture on a piece of wadding and position a piece of thin backing fabric behind. Pin and tack around the edges.

4. Sew around the brick or stone shapes, stitching through all three layers to obtain a quilted wall effect.

Rooftops

Look at the rooftops of the surrounding area. Are they all made from the same materials? We normally see roofs from a viewpoint on the ground. Is there a vantage point from which you can see them from a different viewpoint? Look at the angles of the roofs. Talk about pitch. Why don't buildings always have flat roofs? Look at the patterns presented by the juxtaposition of the various roofs. Consider how you could make an interesting card or clay roofscape.

Card Relief Roofscape

Resources
- Carton card
- Corrugated card
- Thin background card
- PVA glue
- Paint

Approach

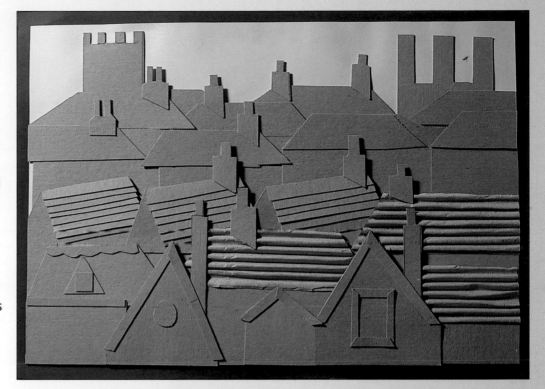

1. Look carefully at photographs of rooftops, noting the angles and textures of the roofs.

2. On thin carton card draw the outlines of the rooftops that will make up the skyline.

3. Cut them out and glue them into position on the background card.

4. Draw and cut out the next row of rooftops and glue these down so that they overlap the first row.

5. Proceed in this manner towards the bottom edge of the background card.

6. Finally cut out details such as chimneystacks, roof tiles, window frames and weatherboarding, and apply these to the buildings. Paint if desired when dry.

Clay Relief Roofscape

Resources
- Clay
- Slip
- Clay tools

Approach

1. Roll out a slab of clay between two wooden guides to ensure an even thickness (1.5 to 2cm).

2. Cut out a rectangle of clay for the background.

3. Roll the remaining clay slightly thinner and cut out a number of roof shapes.

4. Proceed to build up the roofscape as for the card relief roofscape, remembering to join the pieces of clay with slip or a little water.

5. The roofs can be decorated either by impressing with a clay tool or by rolling and pressing little beads of clay to create separate tiles and then attaching them to the roof using slip.

6. Treetops can be positioned amongst the roofs to add more interest. Rooftops can be lifted slightly by inserting thin sausages of clay beneath them for support.

Urban Sunsets

Buildings and rooftops silhouetted against the rich colours of a sunset make a very striking image and provide a stimulus for dramatic artwork in paint and cut-and-torn paper. The light changes very rapidly as the sun sets, so it is worth taking several photographs of the same view. Because of the intensity of the background light, objects in the foreground will often become dense black, hiding all visible detail.

Monoprints and Pen

Resources
- White drawing paper
- Sheets of transparent plastic or off-cuts of melamine or laminated board
- Ready-mixed paint
- Brushes
- Drawing paper
- Black felt-tipped pens

Approach

1. Mark out an area on the board the same size as the paper or, if using transparent plastic, slip another sheet of paper underneath as a guide.

2. Squirt out a line of black paint just above the bottom edge of the marked area.

3. A little way above this, squirt a line of yellow or orange paint.

4. Proceed in this way until all the required colours have been laid down.

5. Using a brush, lightly spread the lines of colour until they meet.

6. Carefully lower a sheet of paper onto the paint and press down firmly. Smooth across the paper with the palm of the hand.

7. Gently peel the paper off the board and leave to dry. There may be sufficient paint left to take off another print.

8. When the print is dry, use black felt-tipped pens or paint to draw in the rooftops and outlines of buildings.

Paper Sunsets

Resources
- White drawing paper
- Black paper
- Tissue paper in sunset colours
- Cellulose paste

Approach

1. Paste torn strips of coloured tissue paper onto white drawing paper to create a sunset sky.

2. On black paper draw a continuous skyline from one side of the paper to the other (include chimney tops, trees, roofs, church spires, television aerials and so on).

3. Cut out the skyline and paste onto the bottom section of the tissue sky.

Variation
Paint a colour-wash background instead of using tissue and proceed as above.

Sunset over Water

Uncluttered views of sunsets over expanses of water make excellent starting points for tapestry weavings as very little shaping is required. Try to include a sparkling light path reflected in the water. This creates an impression of depth and gives a focus to the scene. In addition to photographs, collect appropriate images from newspapers, magazines or travel brochures.

Sunset Weavings

Resources
- Photographs of sunsets
- Carton card
- Coloured wools
- Weaving or large-eyed needles
- Short lengths of dowel or cane

Approach

Warping

1. To make a card loom cut the carton card to the required size, allowing an extra 2cm on the width and length.

2. Mark the top and bottom edges of the card at 1cm intervals.

3. Cut slits in the card at these marks to a depth of 1cm.

4. Attach the warp thread to the card loom by winding several times around the first 'tooth', then bring the wool to the front of the card through the first slit.

5. Take it down to the bottom of the card, through the first slit, behind the 'tooth' and out through the second slit.

6. Now take the wool up to the top of the card and into the second slit, behind the 'tooth' and out through the third slit.

7. Continue in this way until the loom is warped.

8. Finish by winding the wool several times around the last 'tooth'.

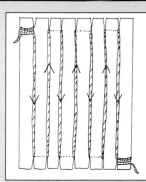

Warping a card loom

Weaving

1. Thread the weaving or large-eyed needle and weave several rows in one colour. Then, in order to create the ripple effect, add another colour to the wool already in the needle and work several more rows.

2. A third colour may be added at this point so that you are actually weaving with three different-coloured wools in the needle at the same time.

3. Gradually change colour by dropping the first strand of wool and perhaps adding another colour to the two remaining in the needle.

4. Always join new lengths of wool at a point near the middle of the line of weaving – never at the end of a row. Joining at the end makes the edges weak and untidy. Push the end of the length of wool to the back of the work, count back three or four warp threads and join the new length at this point, repeating the under–over pattern of the previous row. Once past the join, the pattern will be correct.

5. Take care not to pull the wool tightly at the edges of the work or the weaving will narrow. Always leave a little loop at the edge so that the wool is not pulling against the last warp thread.

6. When the work is complete, slip the weaving off the card by bending the 'teeth' forwards and slipping the wool from behind.

Joining new yarn

7. Slip lengths of dowel through the loops at the top and bottom of the weaving for hanging. Add a fringe if desired.

Winter Streets

Take photographs of the local area in various weather and lighting conditions as a starting point for work on shade, tone and texture. Try to capture street furniture such as lampposts, signs, bus shelters and telephone boxes. Trees or people can also add interest to a winter scene.

Street Scenes

Resources
- Grey and blue paper
- Black wax crayons
- White and yellow chalk

Approach

1. Using a thin black wax crayon, draw a winter scene on grey paper, taking care to include such details as tree trunks, lampposts or figures.

2. Lightly shade other areas such as rooftops. It is important to maintain the balance between light and dark areas.

3. When the drawing is complete, highlight areas with white chalk. Use the chalk sparingly.

4. Use yellow chalk to light up the occasional window or street lamp.

Variation

Create a night street scene by using blue paper instead of grey. Introduce a little more yellow chalk by colouring in more windows and car headlights.

Fabric Collage

Resources
- Scraps of wool, braid, fringing
- Wintry coloured fabrics, including white and blue satins, brown needle cord, fur fabrics and velvets
- PVA glue

Approach

1. Draw a plan of the winter scene.

2. Starting at the top of the card, glue on strips of fabric to create a sky effect.

3. Gradually work down the card, piecing together the winter background.

4. Once this is complete, add detail such as trees, walls, fences, houses and roads.

Frosted Foliage

Scenes that we take for granted and that go largely unnoticed in the normal course of events are amazingly transformed by a sprinkling of snow or a thick hoar frost. What was once a scrubby patch of grass and a few straggly bushes can become a magical wonderland of new shapes and patterns, and a source of real inspiration for drawing, painting and textile work.

Frosted Foliage

Resources

- Fabrics and threads in white, silver, black, grey and blue
- Scraps of green satin or velvet
- White and silver net
- Smooth and textured black, white and grey wools
- Sequins
- Fabric glue
- Frosted twigs

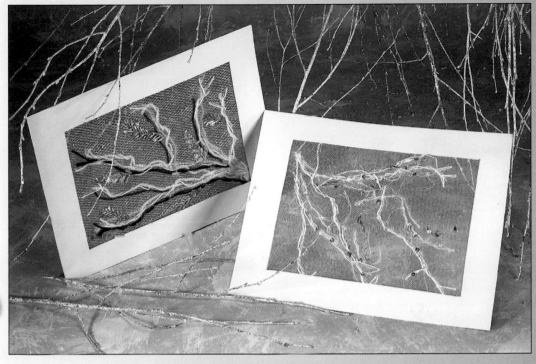

Approach

Frosted Twigs

1. Arrange lengths of textured wool on a piece of net.

2. Place another piece of net over this and pin around the edges and between the wool.

3. Using either embroidery thread or smooth wool, sew along the lines of trapped wool, making sure that everything is held in position.

4. Sew sequins along the lines of the branches.

Frosted Leaves

1. Cut leaf shapes from green velvet or satin and, using a very small amount of glue, stick them to a piece of white satin.

2. Pin a piece of white net over this.

3. Using embroidery thread, sew around each leaf shape (sewing through the white satin, not the green).

4. Carefully snip away the centre of each piece of net, which is covering the leaves.

5. Weave thick, smooth wool under the stitches around each leaf.

6. Mount the net embroideries in open card mounts and display so that the light passes through them. This gives a very wintry effect.

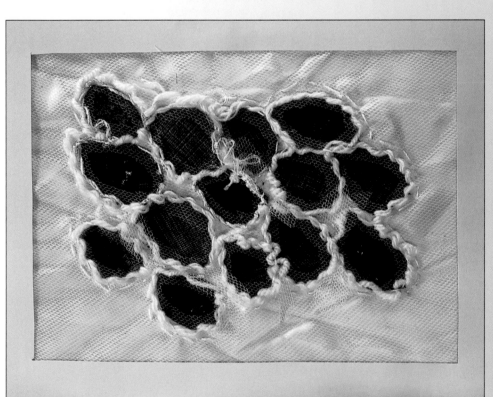

Looking for Lines

Line is a basic element of any pattern work. Before embarking upon line design, it is a good idea to observe and record instances of line patterns in the local environment. Look at things from unusual angles. Use a card viewer to isolate interesting arrangements of lines from the wider background. Use a camera to make a permanent record of findings.

Black and White Line Design

Resources
- White drawing paper
- Selection of writing tools:
  - black felt-tipped pens with a selection of tips, from bullet to italic
  - ballpoint pens
  - thin, pointed wax crayons
  - pencil crayons
  - sketching pencils

Approach

1. As the rectangle is probably the most repeated shape in the immediate environment, it makes a good starting point for this exercise.

2. With the aid of a ruler, draw one rectangle on a piece of white drawing paper.

3. Relate other rectangles to this one, varying the size, thickness of line and proximity, sometimes making one appear to be inside, above or behind the other.

4. When the page is full of empty rectangles, pattern them by drawing in a mixture of freehand and ruler lines, dots, circles and squiggles using a variety of writing tools.

5. This idea could be developed to create imaginary townscapes.

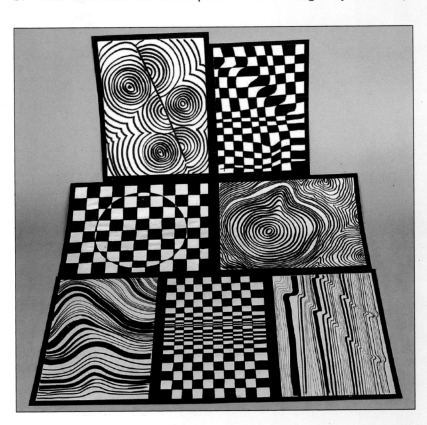

Op Art

Resources
- White drawing paper
- Black felt-tipped pens with a selection of tips, from bullet to italic

Approach

1. Look at the black and white line designs of Bridget Riley, Wolfgang Ludwig, Victor Vasarély and the black and white fabrics used by André Courrèges in the Sixties.

2. Make straight line or wavy patterns flow across the paper, varying their thickness and proximity.

3. Experiment with a chequerboard pattern by introducing a bend into the lines at a given point. Make the paper appear to undulate by introducing blips into the line pattern.

Ancient Architecture

Patterns in ancient architecture can be an exciting stimulus for creative artwork. Compare these patterns to ones found locally. Is modern architecture more or less ornate than ancient architecture? Why do you think this is? Compare patterns found in different periods of architecture. Have architects through the ages been influenced by ancient architecture?

Tissue and Wax Designs

Resources
- White paper
- Tissue paper in stone colours
- Cellulose paste
- Black wax crayons or oil pastels

Approach

1. Study a variety of different architectural patterns.

2. Paste torn strips of tissue paper onto white background paper, making sure that all the edges are securely pasted down. Different depths of colour will be created where the tissues overlap. Cover the whole sheet of paper. Leave to dry.

3. Use a black wax crayon or oil pastel to draw bands of pattern onto the tissue background.

4. When complete, use the side of the crayon or pastel to rub lightly all over the work. The wrinkles in the tissue will pick up the crayon, giving a textured and aged effect.

Wax Scratch-Back Patterns

Approach

Resources
- White paper
- Wooden skewer or stylus for scratching off the wax
- Newspapers
- Orange and black wax crayons

1. Cover the work area with newspapers. Fold a piece of paper in half and, starting at the folded edge, draw half a vase shape, finishing again at the fold.

2. Hold the folded paper together and cut around the drawn shape.

3. Open out the two halves of paper to reveal a complete vase shape.

4. Crayon firmly all over the vase with orange wax crayon. Do not leave any white areas.

5. Next, crayon heavily all over the orange wax with a black wax crayon.

6. Finally, use a wooden stylus to draw the patterns from ancient architecture onto the vase, scratching through the black wax. Whole areas of black wax can be scratched away to reveal glowing areas of orange.

Note: This is an excellent way of depicting patterns from ancient pottery as it mimics the methods used by potters who scratched through the coloured slips applied to the pottery.

Patchwork of Fields

Aerial photographs reveal the wonderful colours and patterns of fields, networks of roads and clusters of houses and villages. Make a collection of similar images as a starting point for work on pattern, colour and texture. Note the combination of curved and straight lines and the way in which some lines seem to meander across the page. Consider where roads might go and what you might see if travelling along a particular road. Develop imaginary maps and paint scenes from journeys.

Textile Field and Village Pattern

Resources
- Green background fabric
- Scraps of fabric in assorted textures and field colours
- Braids, fringing, buttons and beads
- Sewing thread
- Latex fabric glue

Approach

1. Design a field and village landscape.

2. Cut narrow strips of fabric for the roads and glue into position on the background fabric. Use the glue sparingly.

3. Cut out the various field shapes and glue around the area where the village is planned.

4. Sew on beads and buttons of various sizes to represent the buildings of the village and outlying farms.

5. Complete the picture by gluing on braid and fringing to represent walls and woodland.

Taking a Line for a Walk

Resources
- Drawing paper
- Black fine-line pens

Approach

1. Let your eye wander on a journey around the classroom, observing the many features and objects.

2. Using black, fine-line pens on white paper, take a line for a walk around the classroom, drawing all the features observed.

3. Attempt to do this without lifting the pen off the paper.

Note: The idea of taking a line for a walk was used by 20th century artist Paul Klee. He realised that by introducing an element of play into a task, more visually exciting work could result.

Circles All Around

Look for patterns in the environment made up entirely of circles. These might include bales of hay in a field, piles of felled trees in the woods, or a bicycle chained to a railing. Many interesting patterns can be made using circles, and circles can be used as a stimulus to develop work on surface pattern.

Simple Circle Patterns

Resources
- White drawing paper
- Black paper
- Compasses or circular objects around which to draw
- Rulers
- Coloured pencils

Approach

1. Draw an arrangement of circles of different sizes on white paper. Overlap some and divide others with ruled lines.

2. Divide some circles by drawing in the diameter, others by drawing numerous radii. Extend some of these lines across other circles.

3. Colour in all the various segments of the circles using coloured pencils.

4. Cut out the finished interlocking circular design and mount on black paper.

String Bales

Resources
- Card
- Corrugated card
- String, garden twine and thin rope
- Latex or PVA glue

Approach

1. Prepare a textured background by gluing corrugated card onto a piece of smooth card.

2. Coil up the end of a length of string into a spiral and glue this into position. Spread glue around it and continue to coil the string into a larger spiral.

3. Repeat using different types of string and creating different-sized circles.

4. Outline each arrangement with contrasting coloured string or twine.

Machines

Make a collection of images showing the components of agricultural, mining or construction machinery such as engines, cogs, gears, fan belts, pistons, caterpillar tyres and hydraulics. Discuss which parts of the machine might move. Consider how you might attempt to portray this in 2D and relief work.

Moving Cut-Paper Designs

Resources
- White, black, grey and red paper
- Compasses or circular objects around which to draw
- Paper-fasteners
- Glue

Approach

1. Identify the various components of machines.

2. Make a plan of an imaginary machine in sketchbooks.

3. Consider which parts are going to move.

4. Cut out the various parts of the machine and lay them out on the background paper before gluing into position.

5. Use paper-fasteners to attach the moving pieces.

Card Machine Reliefs

Resources
- Carton card
- Thin card
- Glue guns or PVA glue
- Card tubes
- Compasses or circular objects around which to draw
- Metallic spray paint
- Ready-made discs

Approach

1. Draw a plan of a machine relief.

2. Cut a piece of carton card for the background.

3. From thinner card cut out cogs and discs or use ready-made shapes.

4. Assemble these onto the background card in the form of a machine, using short lengths of card tube to raise them to different heights.

5. Glue into position and spray with silver paint when dry.

Textile Patterns

A collection of textiles from different cultures and periods of history makes an excellent starting point for developing individual textile designs. Wherever possible, handle the textiles to feel the textures and examine the stitching. Are the patterns on the textiles made up of simple shapes? Are the shapes repeated, rotated or overlapped?

Embroidered Wall-Hanging

Resources
- Black cotton fabric
- Embroidery threads in a variety of colours and thicknesses
- Tapestry or knitting wools
- Large- and small-eyed needles
- Sequins and beads
- Dark-coloured background fabric

Approach

1. Look carefully at a variety of textile images and samples to examine the colours and types of stitching.

2. Draw a simple embroidery plan, considering which stitches could be used.

3. Cut pieces of fabric about 20 x 25cm. Do not make them too large or they will take too long to sew.

4. Turn a hem all the way round the fabric and sew down in running stitch using a brightly coloured thread.

5. A contrasting colour can then be threaded under these stitches.

6. Draw guidelines onto the fabric using white pencil crayon.

7. Effective patterns can be built up using different combinations of long and short stitches.

8. Add sequins and beads to enhance the pattern.

9. When the embroideries are complete, sew them onto the background fabric and enhance with hand or machine stitching.

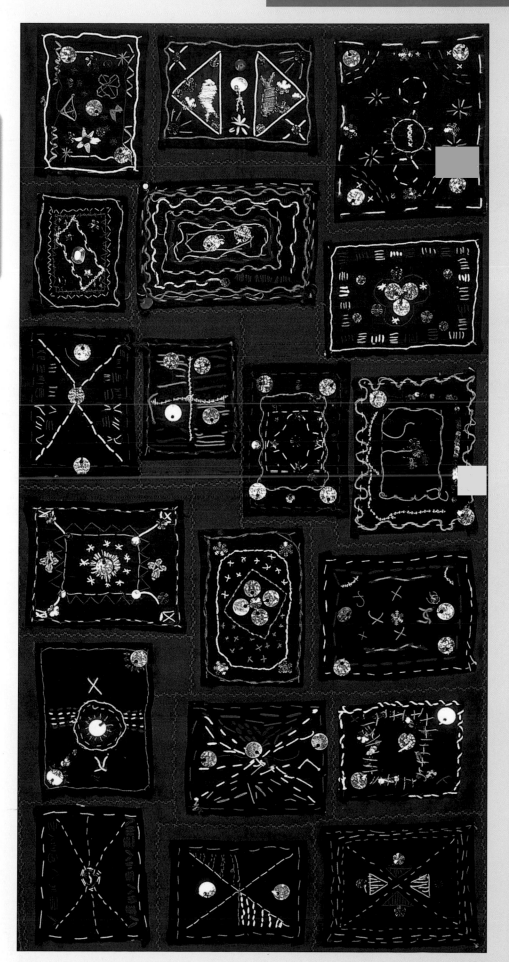

33

Plant-Form Patterns

Studying plant forms can develop an awareness of pattern. See how shapes are repeated many times throughout a plant. Do these shapes remain the same size or are they larger at the top or bottom of the plant? Do the shapes of the leaves or flowers vary or remain constant? Compare how the colours vary from one part of the plant to another. Develop growth patterns using these repeated shapes and consider how to create the impression of texture using only marks and lines.

Growth Patterns

Approach

1. Look at the interesting leaf and flower shapes of a variety of plants.

2. Begin by drawing a simple shape on the bottom edge of the paper. Starting from any point on the edge of this shape, draw a repeated shape, finishing again at the bottom edge of the paper.

3. Continue adding 'growths' to the plant, working first on one side and then the other, until the whole paper is filled.

4. Remember to change the colour and thickness of the line as it progresses. Limit the colours to a range of greens and yellows.

5. Using solid colour, lines, spots, squiggles and shading, fill in each area of the pattern, taking care to maintain a balance between filled-in and open areas of the work. Use as a colour-mixing exercise if using paint.

Variation

Use the same idea to create a textile collage, incorporating plain and patterned fabrics and interesting textures.

Resources

- A wide variety of writing tools in a limited range of colours:
  - thin and broad felt-tipped pens
  - pointed wax crayons
  - gel pens
  - ballpoint pens
  - paintbrushes

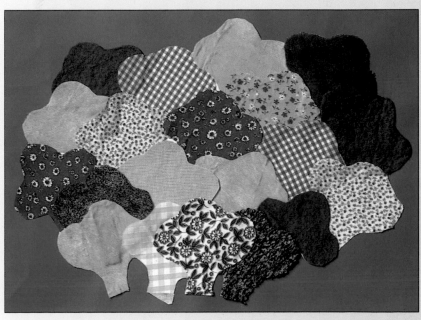

Foliage

Large, clear leaf shapes and areas of dense foliage provide a good starting point for work on printing and pattern. Examine the work of the late 19th-century, early 20th-century French designer E A Seguy to see how simple plant shapes are used to create very colourful and dramatic designs. Also look at the work of William Morris to see how plant forms were used to inspire printed patterns for wallpaper and fabric.

String Prints

Resources
- Large sheets of white drawing paper
- Carton card
- Thick, smooth string
- PVA glue
- 25mm decorator's brush
- Paints
- Paintbrushes
- Print rollers

Approach

1. Make a printing block by gluing together several pieces of carton card.

2. Onto this, draw a leaf or flower shape.

3. Glue on the string using the drawn lines as a guide.

4. Cover the whole block with PVA glue as this makes it stronger and easier to wipe clean. Leave to dry.

5. Use the decorator's brush to create a colourwash background on large sheets of drawing paper. Leave to dry.

6. Wind string around the print roller. Secure the ends with masking tape and brush the paint onto the string (this is more accurate and less messy than rolling into a tray of paint).

7. Roll from the bottom to the top of the paper to create vines or stems.

8. Paint the string on the card printing blocks and print leaves or flowers along the stems.

Paint Speckling

Resources
- White paper
- Paints
- Paintbrushes
- Thin card
- Toothbrushes

Approach

1. Lightly colourwash the background paper.

2. From card, cut out simple leaf and flower shapes of different sizes. You will need quite a few.

3. Consider where the flowers are going to be and speckle these areas first. Dip the tips of the toothbrush bristles into the paint, then angle the toothbrush downwards towards the paper and with the forefinger of the free hand gently stroke the bristles. Build up a layer of specks of paint.

4. Arrange the card flowers over this to mask areas of speckling.

5. Speckle other areas green and position some leaves. Speckle around these shapes with a darker tone.

6. Position more leaves overlapping others and continue to build up the pattern in this way.

7. Remove the card shapes when the paint is dry and add flower centres with a fine paintbrush.

Meadow Grass

Photographs of grasses and meadow flowers can be a starting point for interesting stitching. Daisies and dandelions in an open field, grasses growing against a wall or weeds growing up between paving stones, all make good starting points for creative embroidery.

Meadow Grass Embroideries

Approach

1. Pull threads from around the rectangle of background material to create a fringe and to prevent further fraying.

2. Look closely at photographs of meadow grasses and note the directional lines. These could be marked on the fabric with a fine felt-tipped pen.

3. Start by sewing quite large straight stitches along these lines. Add smaller stitches between these, building up a layer of stitches in different shades of thread.

4. Look at the shapes of the flowers. Represent the flowers with stitches or by sewing on tiny fabric flowers. To create the pink grass heads, simply sew long stitches in a soft, hairy knitting wool.

Resources
- Loosely woven background fabrics such as coloured or natural hessian
- Wide selection of embroidery threads
- Tapestry and knitting wools
- Small flower heads from fabric flowers
- Large-eyed tapestry needles
- Fine felt-tipped pens

Flowers

There is no doubt that artists throughout history, from Albrecht Dürer to Georgia O'Keeffe, have been inspired to paint flowers, sometimes a single bloom, sometimes a whole field of flowers. Look closely at flowers and notice the way that they are constructed. Feel the texture of the petals, stalk and leaves. Are they soft and silky, smooth and glossy, sharp and spiky or rough and hairy? Capture these characteristics through observational drawings and paintings, and develop them into a freer, more impressionistic style. Compare the flower paintings of Monet and Van Gogh to those of Dürer and O'Keeffe. Consider viewpoint, scale, colour and brushstrokes. What is it about flowers that artists are trying to capture?

Paper Batik

Approach

1. Using wax crayons, draw and colour flowers. Add a suitable wax background. It is very important to press on heavily with the crayon and colour the whole sheet of paper. Any paper not waxed will absorb the dark ink or dye.

2. Crumple the picture into a loose ball, taking care to crack the wax.

3. Smooth out the picture and, wearing protective gloves, brush well with ink, working it into the creases. Wipe off the excess ink with tissues.

4. Place the picture face down on a wad of newspaper and iron lightly to flatten.

 Note: Children must be supervised when using a hot iron.

Resources
- Cartridge paper
- Dark-coloured ink or fabric dye
- Protective gloves
- Newspaper
- Wax crayons
- Paintbrushes
- Tissues
- Iron

Pods and Seed Heads

Photographs of pods, seed heads and unusual plants can provide inspiration for creating interestingly shaped containers. A visit to the local garden centre may offer the opportunity to observe more unusual and exotic collections of plants for this purpose.

Papier-Mâché Containers

Approach

1. Look carefully at a variety of pod and seed-head shapes.

2. Decide upon a suitable mould to create a papier-mâché container inspired by the seed heads. This could be an inflated balloon or a plastic pudding basin.

3. Paste a layer of torn white paper over the mould, followed by several layers of torn newsprint. The more layers of newsprint, the stronger the finished article will be. Leave to dry.

4. At this stage extra shaping may be added in the form of card collars or coiled newspaper and tube bases.

5. To attach a tube of thin card to a rounded shape snip slits around the bottom edge of the tube and press it down onto the rounded shape. The bottom edge will fan out and can then be taped in place with masking tape. Finish by pasting over with a final layer of white paper.

6. An interesting texture can be achieved by gluing scrunched-up netting around the container. Dip the net in slightly diluted PVA glue and then arrange around the container.

7. Paint when dry.

Resources

- Moulds
- Thin white paper
- Thin card
- Masking tape
- PVA glue
- Newspaper
- Cellulose paste
- Card tubes
- Netting
- Paints

Tree-Bark Textures

The bark of trees offers a fascinating variety of textures and patterns that can be interpreted in many different ways. Look at as many tree trunks as possible and record your observations. Is the surface of the tree smooth, rough, peeling, ridged? Does it have bumps, holes and cracks? How many colours can be seen in the trunk? Are all trees brown?

44

Tree-Bark Textures

Resources
- Scraps of coloured paper
- Tissue paper
- Wood shavings, sawdust and sand
- Paper pulp
- String
- Scraps of hessian
- Cellulose paste or PVA glue
- Paint

Approach

Consider ways of making interesting tree-bark textures. For example:

- Create a textured background with layers of crumpled tissue or thin paper and add string, distressed hessian or scraps of torn paper. Paint in tree-bark colours.

- Mix sand or sawdust with cellulose paste or PVA glue. Fold a piece of background paper vertically to create ridges and spread with sawdust. Paint the textured relief.

- Glue down wood shavings or paper pulp and paint in shades of brown and green.

Stitched Textures

Resources
- Loosely woven fabric such as hessian in brown, green, grey or other natural shades
- Textured wools
- Large-eyed tapestry needles

Approach

1. Pull threads from around a rectangle of hessian to create a fringed border.

2. Pull more threads from the hessian to make channels along which to sew.

3. Weave textured wools along these channels.

4. Pull the fabric out of shape and create holes.

5. Stitch or sew the distressed fabric to a natural-coloured background.

A Woodland Path

A walk through the woods, to the park or along a tree-lined avenue provides excellent photographic opportunities. Record the textures found on paths, mossy banks, tree trunks and in patches of grass. Take photographs directly upwards through the canopy or bare branches of the trees. Different patterns can be recorded with each passing season.

Woodland Path Collage

Resources
- Stiff card
- String
- PVA glue
- Tissue paper
- Wood shavings, sawdust and sand
- Acrylic paints (or powder paints mixed with PVA glue)
- Newspaper
- Cellulose paste

Approach

1. Crumple white tissue paper, ease out and glue to stiff card to create a textured background.

2. Twist up sheets of newspaper to make paper ropes and glue side by side to form a large tree trunk.

3. Glue lengths of string in the centre background to create distant trees.

4. Add another layer of crumpled tissue on top of the string to push the trees into the distance.

5. Twist up tissue paper to make slightly larger, individual tree trunks like those on the right-hand side of the collage.

6. Create grassy banks by gluing down wood shavings or torn and crumpled scraps of thin paper.

7. Create paths by adding sand to thick cellulose paste and spread on using a spatula or old knife.

8. Paint the woodland scene when everything is completely dry.

Winter Trees

Bare trees and branches silhouetted against a wintry sky make a good starting point for a variety of artwork. Look at the direction or flow of the lines. Note the variety of thicknesses and the density of lines. Consider with what media they would be best interpreted.

Textured Trees

Resources
- Thin card
- White tissue paper
- Paints
- Thick string
- Hessian
- PVA glue
- Fine paint brushes

String Trees

Approach

1. Crumple up white tissue paper, then ease it out and glue to card to create a textured background.

2. When dry, paint the top two-thirds in wintry sky colours and the bottom third in black or brown. Leave to dry.

3. Glue on lengths of string to represent tree trunks.

4. Paint the string tree trunks, adding small branches with a fine paintbrush.

Hessian Trees

Approach

1. Prepare the background as above.

2. Take a piece of hessian a bit smaller than the background card and distress it by pulling out threads and generally distorting the shape.

3. Glue to the card, adding the drawn threads to create tree trunks and branches.

4. Add lengths of string if desired and paint when dry.

Ink-blown Trees

Resources
- Drawing paper
- Paints
- Paintbrushes
- Indian ink or black paint
- Drinking straws

Approach

1. Colourwash the background with wintry sky colours.

2. When dry, drop blobs of ink or black paint on the bottom edge of the paper and use a straw to blow them upwards and across the paper to create tree trunks and branches.

3. Keep turning the paper to make the process easier.

4. Paint a band of black along the bottom edge of the paper to create a foreground.

⚠ **Note: Great care must be taken to ensure that the children do not hyperventilate when blowing paint through straws.**

Twisted Trees

Twisted tree trunks, such as the one featured here, make an excellent starting point for 3D work and soft sculpture. Look for the pattern of movement within the trunk. See how the lines flow and entwine, disappear and emerge. Consider how you might interpret such a form as this.

Paper Tree Sculptures

Resources
- Newspapers
- Lengths of card tube about 8–10cm in diameter
- Masking tape
- PVA glue
- Carton card
- Paints

Approach

1. Twist sheets of newspaper into paper 'ropes'.

2. Using masking tape, fasten one end of the newspaper rope over the top edge of a card tube.

3. Glue the length of rope down the side of the tube and trim to size.

4. Repeat this several times, crossing and twisting the ropes over each other.

5. Glue shorter lengths of 'rope' into the spaces.

6. When the tube is covered, glue to a card base.

7. Paint when dry.

Clay Twisted Tree Sculptures

Resources
- Clay
- Card tubes
- Slip

Approach

1. Roll out a slab of clay between two wooden guides to ensure an even thickness (1.5–2cm).

2. Cut out a piece of clay about 15cm square.

3. Wrap the clay around a card tube to create a clay pot shape.

4. Wet the edges of the clay. Join and smooth the edges evenly together. Remove the card tube.

5. From the remaining clay cut out an irregular shape a little larger than the base of the clay pot.

6. Use slip or water to join the clay tube to the base, smoothing the two together.

7. Roll out long, thin sausages of clay and join to the sides of the pot, smoothing the ends over the rim and out onto the base.

8. When dry or fired, either glaze or paint the clay twisted tree sculpture.

Country Landscapes

Photographs are a very useful record of scenes experienced outdoors. They help to capture the form and colours of country landscapes for later use. When photographing landscapes make use of scale and perspective by including a foreground such as a gate, plants or trees. Lead the eye into the picture by including a line of trees, a path or a fence. Look for bands of colour within the scene. An expanse of flat blue sky can be boring but the inclusion of cloud formations can add interest.

Woven Landscapes

Resources
- Card looms or nail frames
- White paper
- Textured wools in greens, browns, yellows, blues and white
- Scraps of fabric in landscape colours
- Twigs, cane or wooden dowelling

Approach

1. Prepare a loom as described for Sunset Weavings on page 17.

2. Cut a piece of white paper small enough to slip under the warp threads.

3. On the paper draw a plan of the landscape to be woven. Stress that this is merely a plan of the weaving and no fine detail is required.

4. Start by weaving several stripes of colour across the whole width of the weaving.

5. Always join new lengths of wool at a point near the middle of the line of weaving, never at the end of a row. Joining at the end makes the edges weak and untidy. (See page 17 Joining new yarn.)

6. Create slopes and hills by weaving one less warp thread on each row on one or both sides. See diagrams (a) and (b).

7. When the whole loom has been filled, slip the weaving off the card and onto lengths of twig, cane or dowelling. Add a fringe if desired.

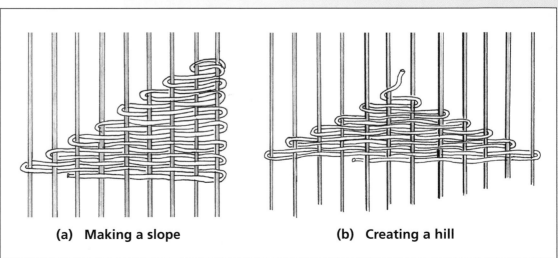

(a) Making a slope   (b) Creating a hill

Paper Lakes

Photographs taken towards the sun, especially over water, sometimes produce dramatic results. Be sure to exclude the sun from the actual viewfinder and, if possible, shade the lens against the glare. The brightness of the background light will throw any foreground detail into black relief. Try to frame the shot with trees or foliage. Use images such as these as the starting point for work on tone.

Monochrome Lakes

Resources
- White drawing paper
- Grey tissue papers
- Silver foil
- Black and grey papers
- PVA glue

Approach

1. Cover the top part of the white drawing paper with pasted strips of torn grey tissue paper.

2. Cut a piece of silver foil to fit the bottom part of the paper.

3. Lightly crumple this and flatten out again. Glue it into position.

4. Cut hill shapes from different shades of grey paper, remembering that the distant hills will be the lightest

5. Cut pieces of black paper to represent the reflections in the water. Fringe the pieces to represent ripples.

6. Frame the view with black paper cutouts of foliage and grass.

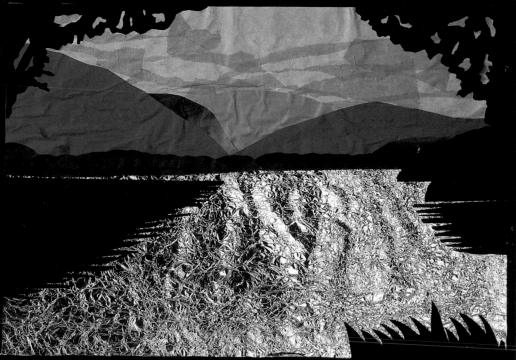

Fabric Lakes

Resources
- Thin card
- Fabric glue
- Grey and black netting
- Silver fabrics
- Fabrics (e.g. chiffon) in shades of grey

Approach

1. Use fabrics to create a lakeland scene.

2. Cut out hill shapes from grey fabric and stick them at the top of the background card.

3. Cover the hills with a layer of chiffon to create a sense of distance and mist.

4. Cut out more hill shapes and place over the chiffon.

5. Use silvery fabric for the water and add grey or black netting to create shadows.

Reflections

Are these photographs the right way up? View them from both angles. How do you know which is the right way? Do you find it disturbing viewing them upside down for a while? Make a collection of similar photographs and images from magazines and travel brochures and use them as starting points for watercolour paintings of reflections in water. Discuss viewpoints and symmetry before starting the paintings.

Paint Blot Landscapes

Resources
- Cartridge paper
- Bottles of ready-mixed paint
- Paintbrushes

Approach

1. Consider the type of scene to be created and plan the order in which colours are going to be laid down, for example a line of brown and then green for a river bank.

2. Fold the paper in half horizontally and then open it out.

3. Squirt a thin line of paint across the paper just above the crease.

4. Leave a gap and then squirt a line of the next colour. Repeat to build up the scene.

5. Using a paintbrush, lightly spread the lines of paint until they almost meet.

6. Fold the bottom half of the paper up and press down onto the paint. Smooth across the paper with the palm of the hand. Pull the two halves apart.

7. Lightly paint in the sky and its reflection when the 'blot' is dry.

Complete the Picture

Resources
- Travel brochures, newspaper supplements, glossy magazines
- Drawing paper
- Glue sticks
- Hand mirrors
- Watercolour paints
- Paintbrushes
- Pencils

Approach

1. Cut out a coloured image from a travel brochure or newspaper supplement that would make a suitable subject for a 'reflections' painting.

2. Glue this onto the top half of the drawing paper.

3. Use a mirror to help work out how the image would be reflected in water and lightly draw this in with pencil.

4. Carefully paint in the reflection and the ripples on the water.

Distorted Reflections

Shiny curved surfaces give a distorted reflection. Look at La Géode, a dome constructed of polished chromium, nickel and steel at the City of Science and Industry just outside Paris. Can you see the distorted reflection of the photographer? Look at yourself in the curved surfaces of stainless steel kettles, teapots, bread or waste bins to see a similarly distorted reflection. The bowls of large shiny spoons can also afford an amusing, distorted reflection.

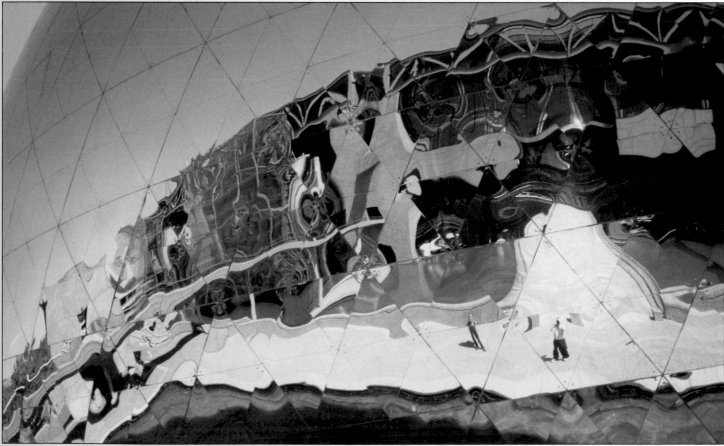

Distorted Faces

Resources
- Large pictures of faces torn from magazines
- Thin card
- Glue sticks
- Lengthened Faces

Approach

Lengthened Faces

1. Cut out a large image of a face from a magazine.

2. Photocopy the image two or three times.

3. Cut the pictures horizontally into strips and reassemble into one lengthened face.

Woven Faces

1. Cut two pictures of the same face or two different faces into strips, one horizontally and the other vertically.

2. Paper-weave the two together.

Multiple Features

1. Take three copies of the same face and cut out the features, such as lips, eyes and noses.

2. Stick these into place, overlapping them slightly to create a repeated image.

3. Cut up the remaining parts of the faces and reassemble them around the features to make one image.

Two-Faced

1. Take two different faces and cut them vertically into uneven sections.

2. Reassemble the face, merging the two images.

Rock Pool

Look for still life arrangements in nature. A trip to the coast or a walk along the shore will reveal many interesting arrangements of rocks, pebbles, shells and flotsam. A rock pool stranded by the retreating tide makes an interesting study of pattern and form.

Rock Pool Tapestry

Resources

- Rug canvas
- Paints
- Paintbrushes
- Wools in rock and seaweed colours
- Large-eyed, blunt-ended needles
- Twigs, driftwood, sea shells with holes, small pebbles
- Scraps of netting
- Thick string
- Scraps of upholstery fringing
- Fabric glue
- Rock-coloured fabric

Approach

1. Cut the rug canvas to size and paint in various shades of grey or rock colours. Leave to dry.

2. To fill in the background, thread two or three strands of different-coloured wools into a needle and stitch in and out of the holes of the rug canvas.

3. Vary the length and direction of the stitch, sometimes missing two or three holes, sometimes four or five. Always come up through the hole next to the one you went down. It is not necessary to cover the whole of the background with stitching.

4. When the central part is covered, you can begin to sew on shells, string, net and bits of driftwood.

5. Attach rocks and pebbles by wrapping them in netting and sewing through the net.

6. Create sea anemones by rolling up and gluing short lengths of upholstery fringe. Alternatively, make a tassel by wrapping wool around a piece of card. Tie a short length of wool through one end of the loops and cut the other end. Tie a piece of wool around the top end of the tassel. Turn upside down and sew to the canvas.

7. To complete, glue or sew the canvas to a piece of rock-coloured background fabric.

Seaweed

The glistening shapes of wet seaweed make an interesting photograph. The repeated shapes of bladderwrack pictured here are reminiscent of the patterns that can be obtained when separating wet-paint papers. The colour range in the photograph is limited but interesting and would make a good starting point for a colour-mixing exercise. Notice how the tips of the seaweed are a lovely golden colour and how certain areas shine white where the light is reflected on the wet surface. Do you think that the sky was grey or blue when the photograph was taken?

Separated Papers

Resources
- Smooth, non-absorbent white paper or thin card
- Cellulose paste
- Paints

Approach

1. Fascinating patterns can be obtained by experimenting with cellulose paste. Much depends upon the thickness of the paste, the amount of paint added and the pressure applied.

2. Mix the paste to a thick consistency and add the paint.

3. Brush the coloured paste thickly over one sheet of paper.

4. Place another sheet of paper over this and press gently.

5. Pull the papers apart diagonally from one corner. Repeat and vary the flow of the pattern by pulling the papers apart from the short side or the long side.

6. Create different patterns by pressing down onto the back of the paper with the fingertips before pulling apart.

7. Try pasting both papers before pressing together and pulling apart.

Paste Combing

Resources
- Smooth, non-absorbent white paper or thin card
- Cellulose paste
- Paints
- Plastic combs, spatulas, spreaders or tools suitable for making marks in the paste
- Newspaper

Approach

1. Mix the cellulose paste to a thick consistency and add the paint.

2. Apply the coloured paste thickly over one sheet of paper and then use a variety of tools to make patterns in the paste.

3. These could be flowing or repeated. Try swirls and spirals.

4. Spread the wet papers out on newspaper to dry.

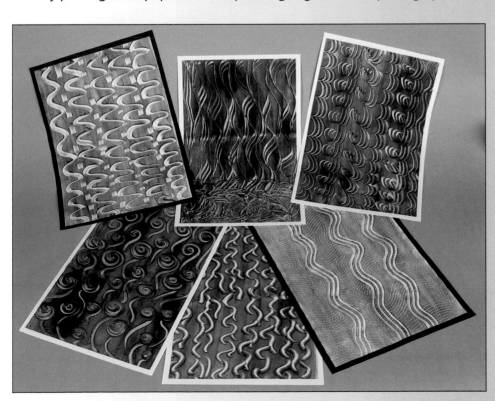

Pebbles

Myriads of soft colours and hues, shapes and forms are to be seen on a pebbly beach. Make a collection of pebbles of different size, form and colour. Handle them and discuss how they feel. Stones with sea-worn holes through them are ready-made sculptures and make an excellent introduction to the work of Barbara Hepworth and Henry Moore.

Plaster Pebble Relief

Resources
- Plaster of Paris
- Clay
- Card box lids
- Pebbles and stones

Approach

1. Roll out the clay to fit inside a box lid. The clay needs to be at least 3cm thick. The lid must be deep enough to accommodate the plaster of Paris on top of the clay.

2. Press the pebbles well into the clay and remove. Make sure that they have left clear indentations.

3. Mix the plaster of Paris according to the instructions on the packet and pour into the lid to a depth of about 4cm. Leave to harden.

4. Carefully peel away the card lid and the clay.

5. Gently clean the surface of the relief and leave to dry thoroughly.

6. Paint if desired.

Plaster Carving

Approach

Resources
- Moulds such as small plastic tubs or packaging from chocolate eggs
- Clay tools, cutlery or other suitable implements with which to carve or make marks in the plaster
- Fine sandpaper

1. Mix the plaster of Paris and fill the moulds to a depth of about 4cm. Half-egg shapes can be filled completely.

2. Remove the plaster shapes from the moulds as soon as they 'go off'.

3. The plaster is best carved while it is still soft inside. If left for too long it will become too hard to carve.

4. Begin to carve the plaster with small spoon handles or clay tools.

5. Once the plaster is too hard to carve, leave it to dry completely and then smooth any rough areas with fine sandpaper.

6. Paint if desired.

Still Life with Jugs

Arrange collections of items into a composition for still life. Consider the viewpoint – place larger items at the back and try to create interesting overlaps. Consider colour and tone. Does one object stand out from another or do they all seem to merge together? What about the background? Does it look busy or confusing? Choose a plain, neutral or contrasting colour for a background drape.

Still Life Collage

Resources
- Plain coloured papers
- Small patterned wallpapers and fabrics
- Pencils
- Felt-tipped pens
- PVA glue

Approach

1. Carefully draw and cut out jugs of different shapes and sizes using the plain and patterned papers and fabrics.

2. Draw jugs on white paper and decorate with felt-tipped pens. Motifs can be drawn and cut out of contrasting coloured papers and used to decorate some jugs.

3. Talk about the foreground and background of the image and consider where the larger jugs should be placed and why.

4. Experiment with various arrangements and layouts of the jugs before gluing them down.

Junk Jugs

Approach

1. Consider the function and design of a jug. What makes it different from a cup? What design elements must a jug have to fulfil its function?

Resources
- Packets, boxes, tubs, card tubes and balloons
- Thin white paper
- Masking tape
- PVA glue
- Paints
- Newspaper
- Thin card
- Coloured paper

2. Create jugs from a variety of box shapes or papier-mâché balloons. Add curved handles by twisting up newspaper into 'ropes' and attaching with masking tape.

3. The pouring lip of the jug could be made from a folded triangle of card taped to the top edge of the box.

4. Once these features have been added, paste torn pieces of paper over the whole jug to strengthen it and cover any newsprint.

5. When dry, paint or cover with a layer of coloured paper.

Collection of Plates

We all love to collect things, from china plates to pebbles or postage stamps. A plate collection could feature floral and geometric patterns and designs from Turkey, Greece, Spain and France, coaching scenes from England and the willow pattern design from China. Use images such as these to develop awareness of pattern from different countries. Talk about your own collections and use collections as starting points for designing your own plates and developing pattern work in blue and white.

Patterning Paper Plates

Resources
- Patterned plates from various countries, cultures and periods of history
- Large paper plates or circles of white card
- Blue ballpoint pens
- Broad and fine felt-tipped pens

Approach

1. Look carefully at the patterns on plates and work out how they are built up. Some will probably be quite geometric in design, others will be free flowing.

2. Some designs, such as the willow pattern, lend themselves to work in ballpoint pen; others with large areas of colour will be better recreated using broad felt-tipped pens.

3. Plan the pattern in sketchbooks before working on the plates.

4. Transfer the pattern to large paper plates or circles of white card.

Pottery Painting

Resources
- Items of white pottery, such as plates, saucers, cups, bowls, jugs
- Water-based ceramic paints
- Fine paintbrushes
- Fine felt-tipped pens

Approach

1. Work out a design in sketchbooks or use the pattern from the paper plate.

2. Using a fine felt-tipped pen of the same colour as the finished design, draw the pattern onto the item of pottery. If mistakes are made they can easily be wiped off with a tissue.

3. When satisfied with the design, use a fine paintbrush to paint on the ceramic paint. (Follow the manufacturer's instructions for drying times and baking.)

Unwanted Snaps

And finally, what do you do with all those snaps that didn't turn out quite as you had hoped? . . . Cut them up and weave with them!

Photo Weaving

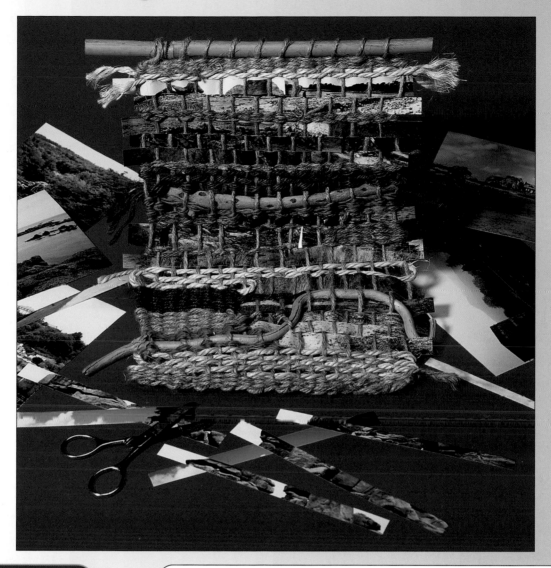

Approach

1. If found objects such as twigs or driftwood are going to be incorporated into the weaving, it is better to use a nail frame rather than a card loom as this allows the objects to lie more easily between the warp threads.

2. A simple nail frame can be made from an old wooden picture frame. Knock in panel pins or small nails at 1cm intervals top and bottom.

3. Warp up the loom with garden twine or string. Weave several rows in this to create a strong, neat edge.

4. Begin to introduce different textures in the form of wools, sliced photographs, or thick string.

5. To fill a whole row with slices of photographs overlap the ends well where they meet.

6. Weave in natural objects such as twigs and pieces of driftwood.

7. For a firm finish, sandwich the rows of photographs between rows of fine weaving.

8. Finish the work with several rows of firm weaving, squeezing in as many as possible.

9. When complete, lift the loops of warp thread from around the nails and slip onto a short length of garden cane.

Resources
- Old photographs sliced into strips
- Garden twine or thin string
- Twigs and driftwood
- Thick, hairy string
- Dowel or garden cane
- Loom
- Natural-coloured wools

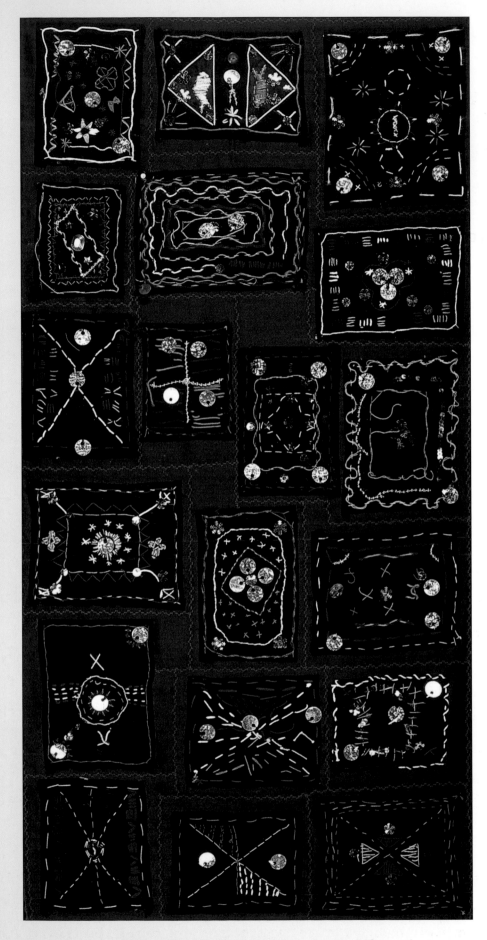

Embroidered Wall-Hanging (page 33)